GORILLA GAMES

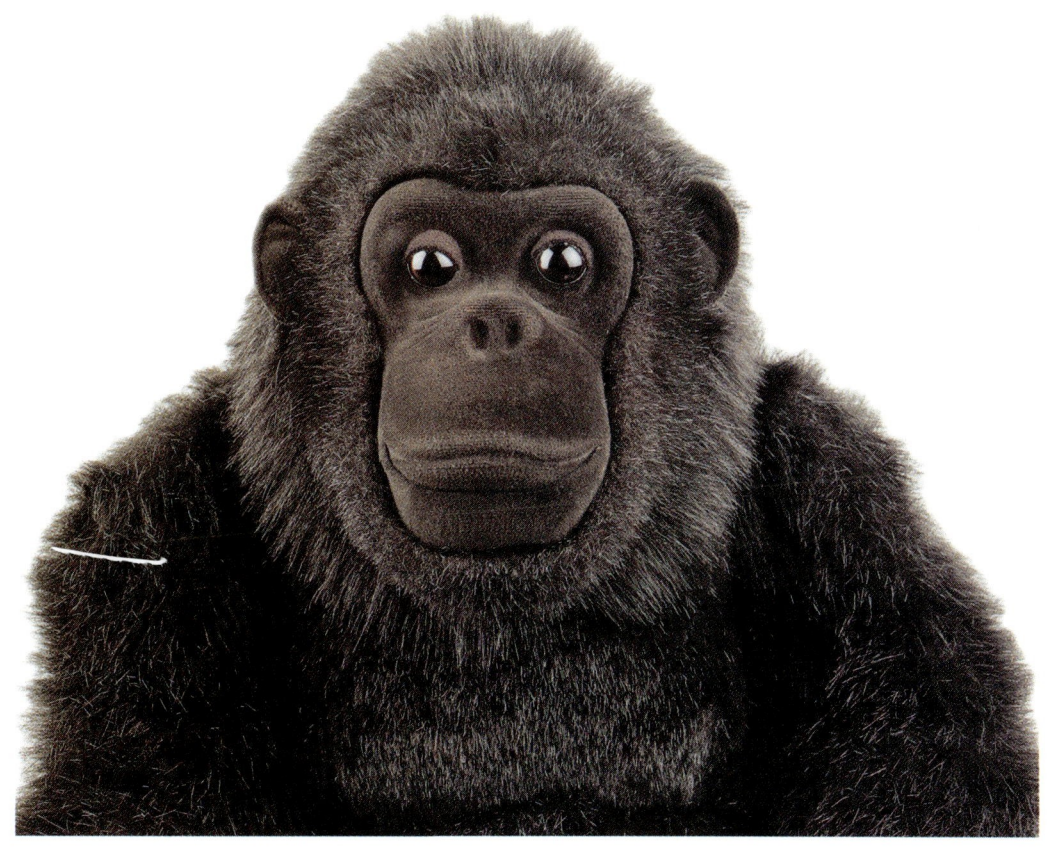

Suzanne Gardner
Photography by Batista Moon Studio

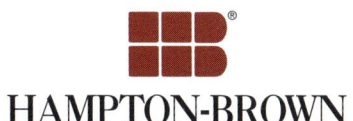

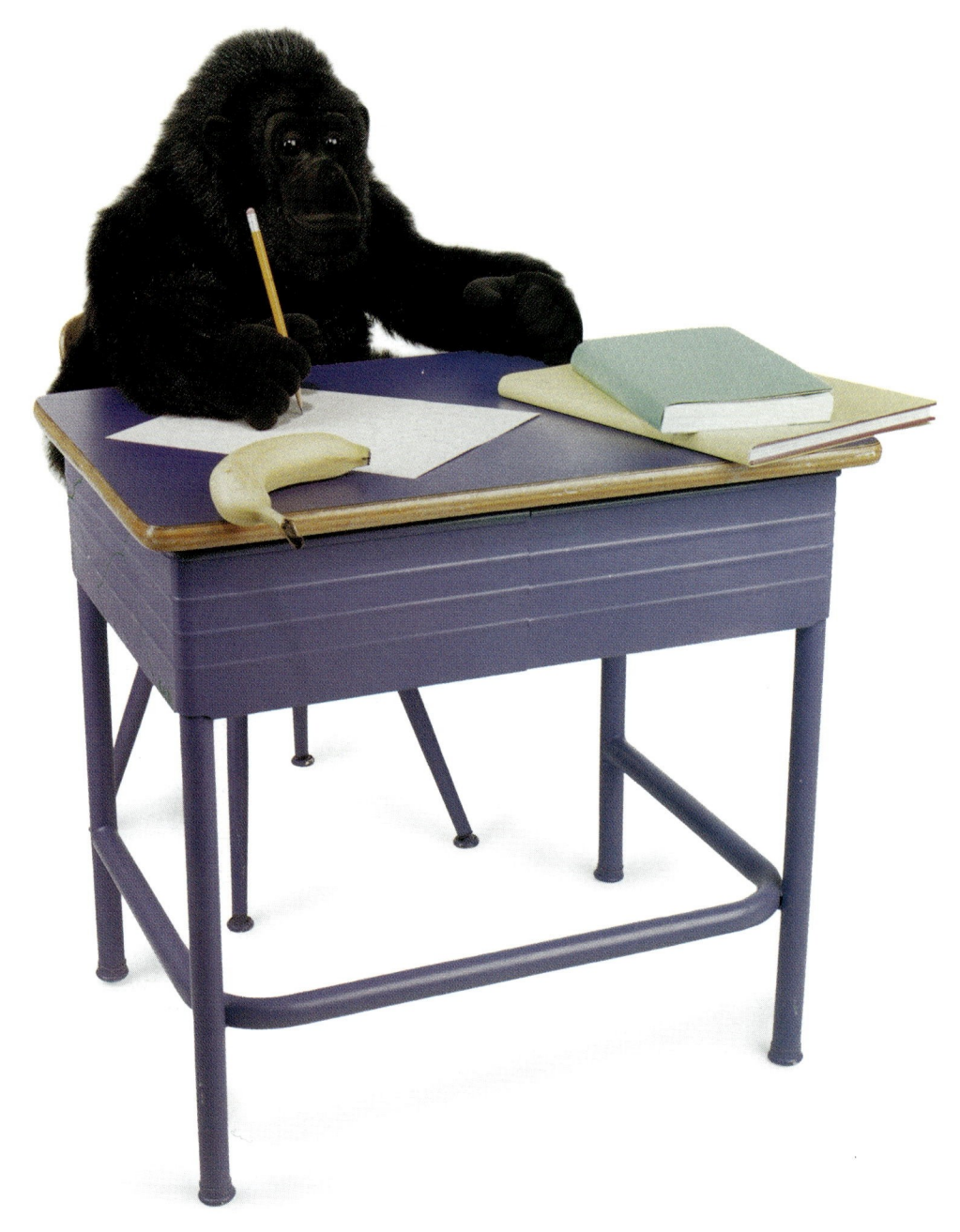

Gorilla goes to school.

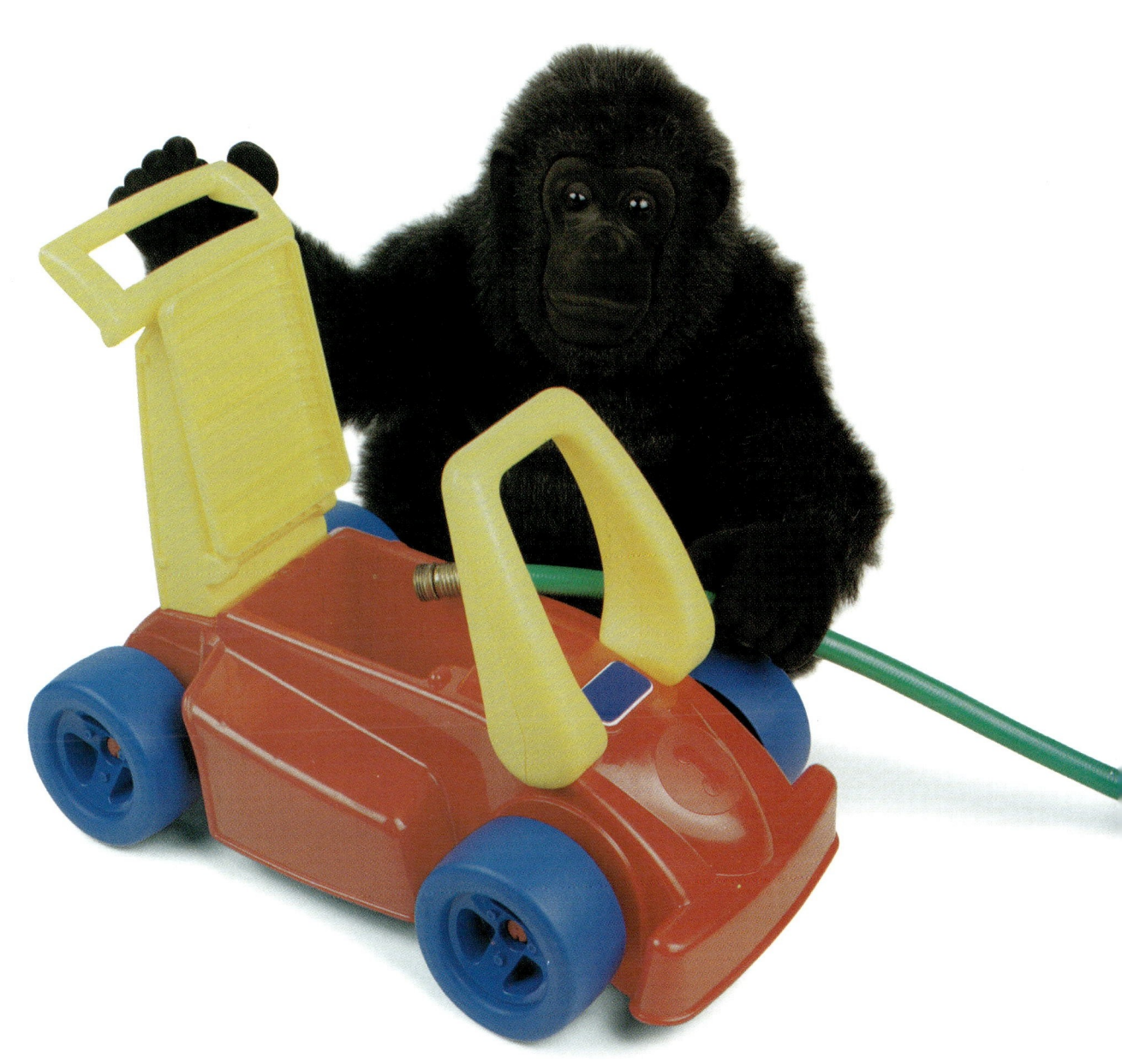

Gorilla goes to the gas station.

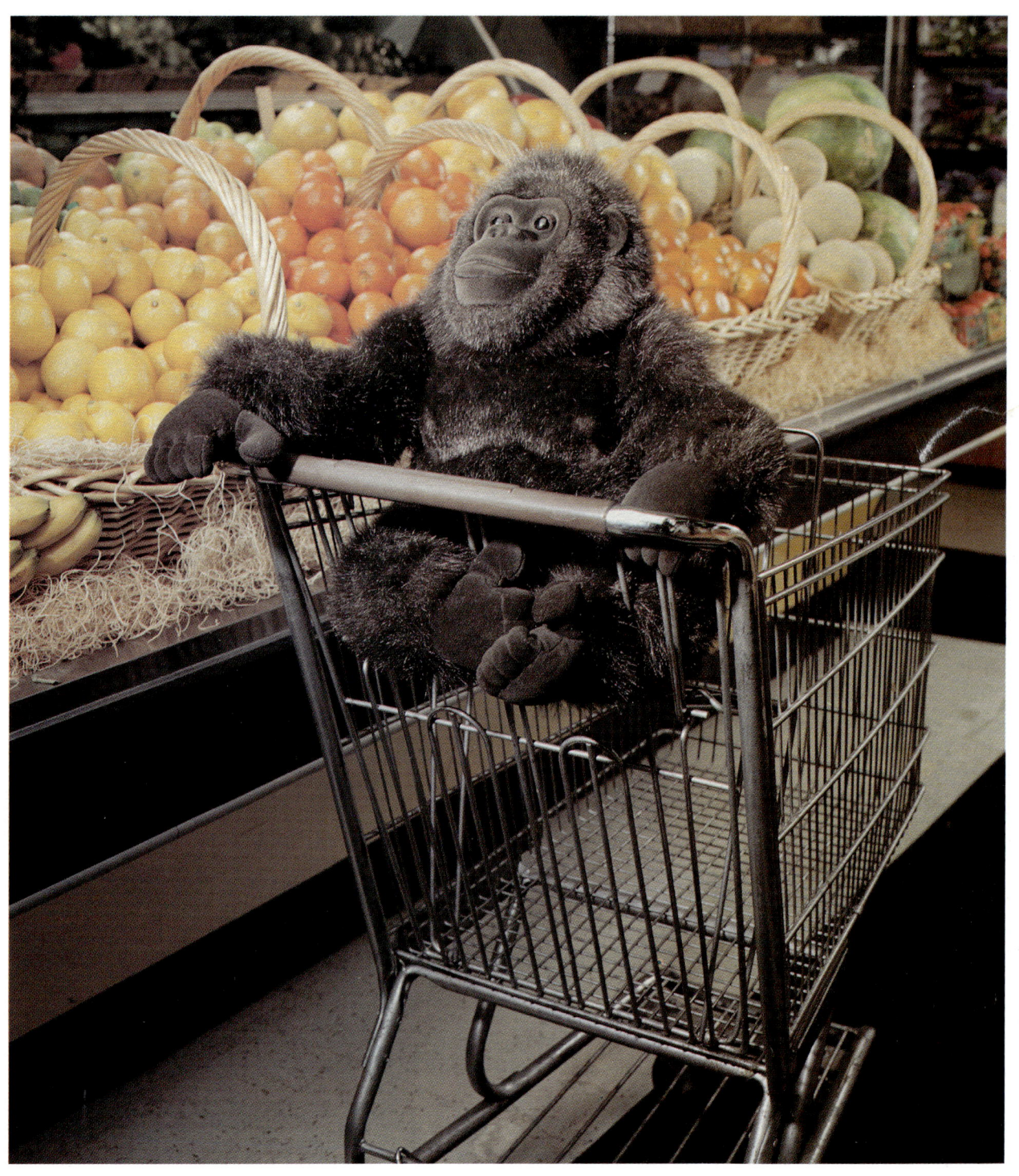

Gorilla goes to the store.

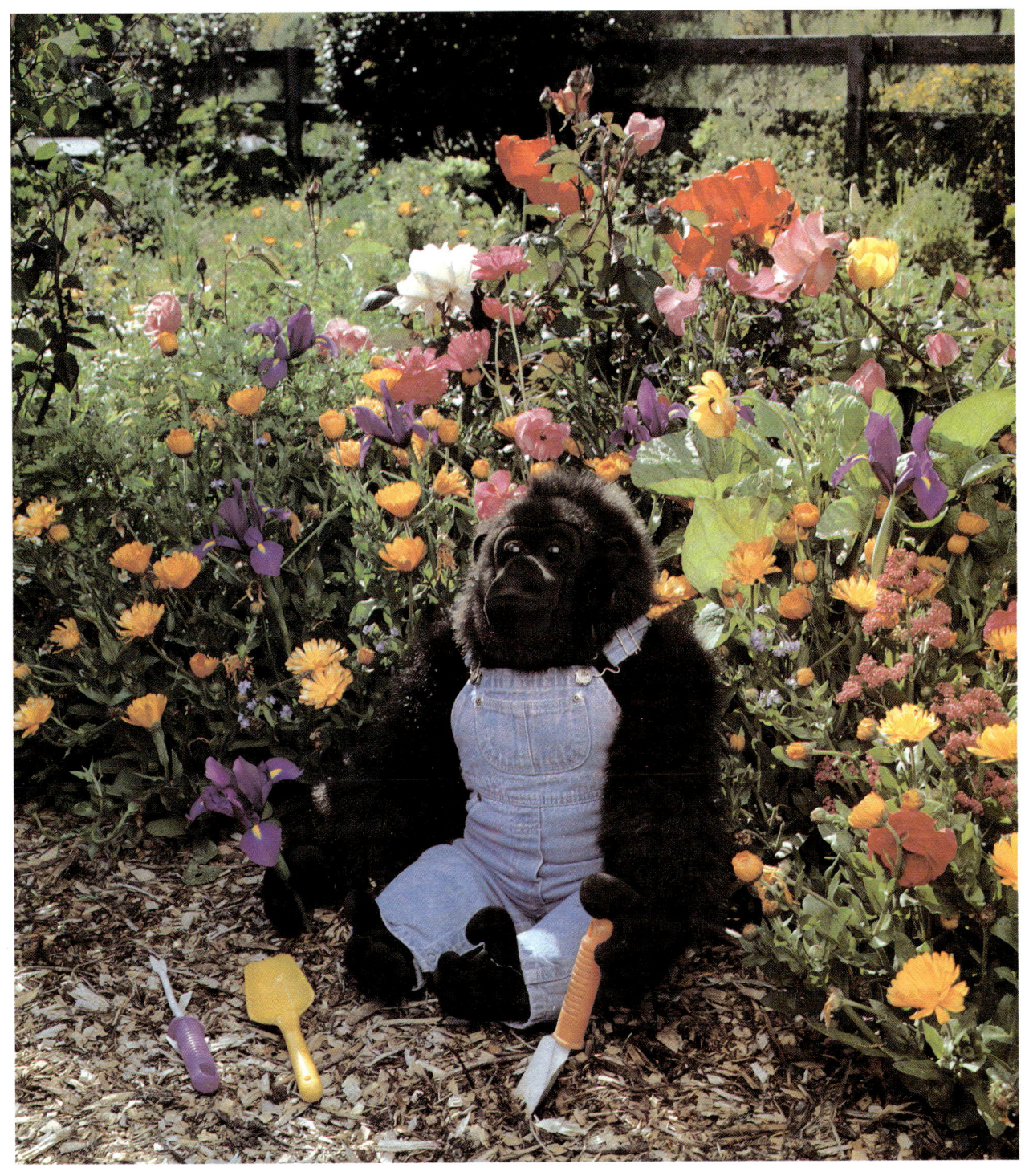

Gorilla goes to the garden.

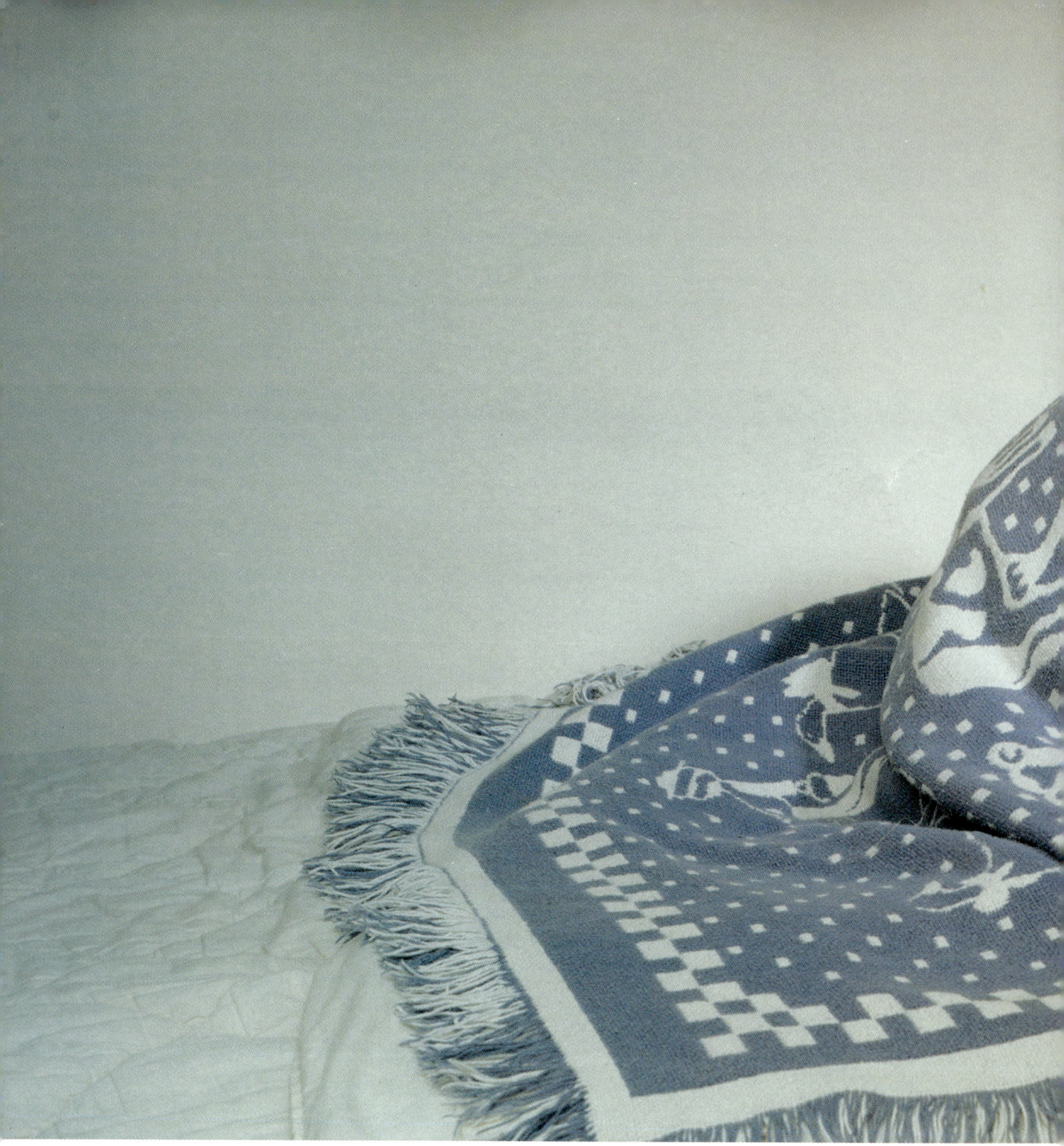

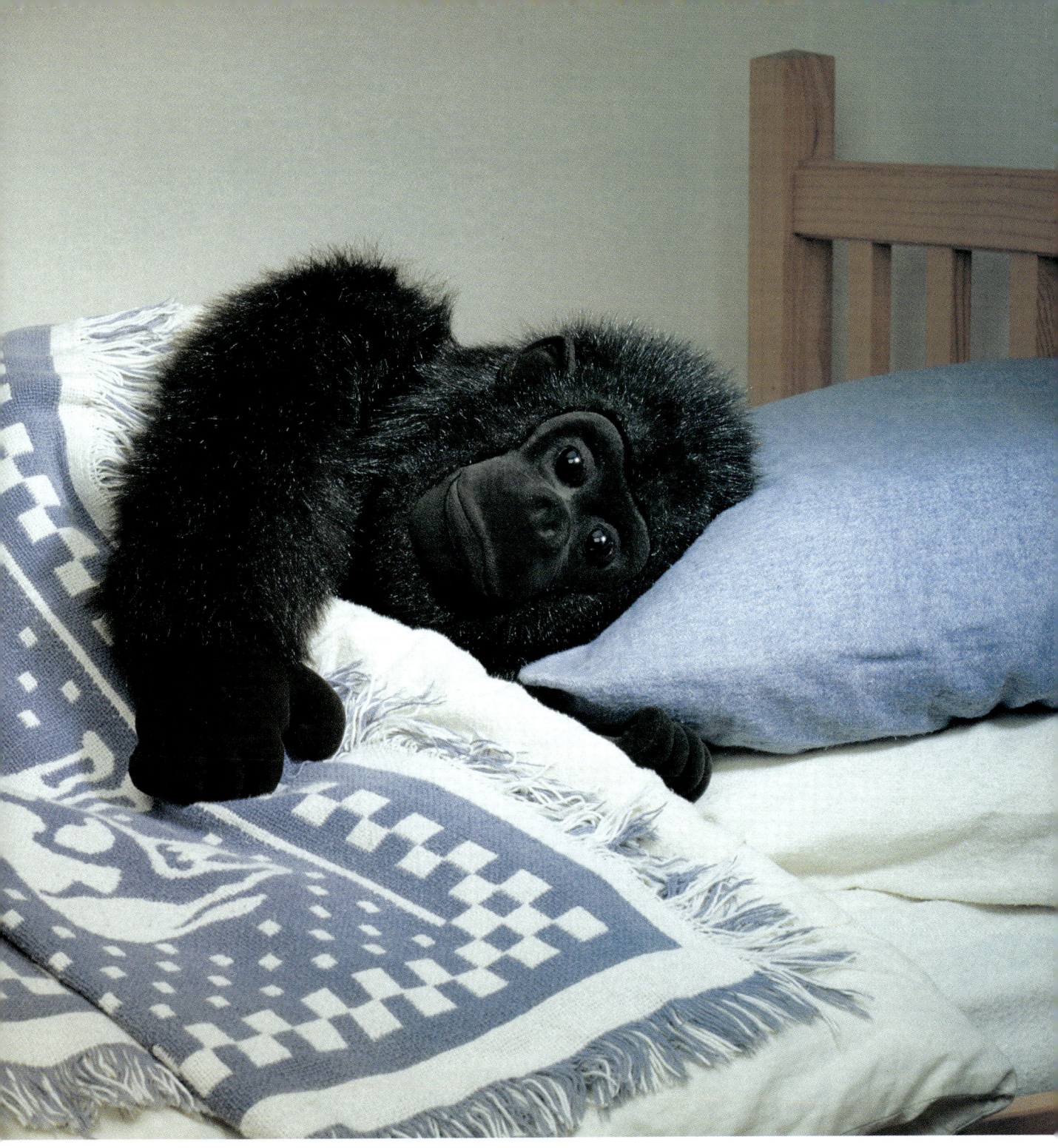

Gorilla goes to bed.

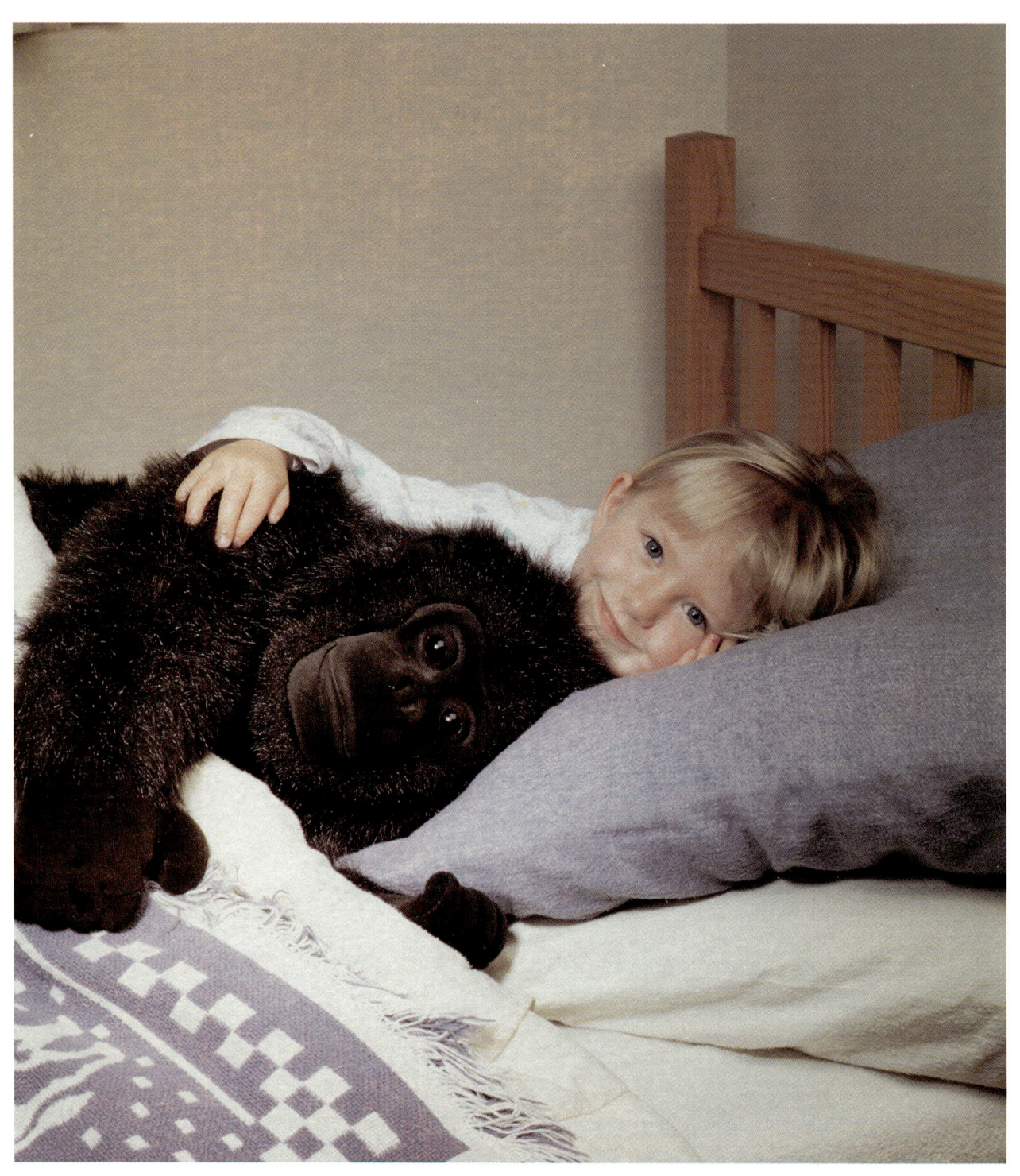

Good night, Gorilla.